The Future of Money

Analyzing Crypto's Massive Impact on the Global Financial System

Table of Contents

Chapter 1. Introduction

In this Special Report, we take a deep dive into the burgeoning world of cryptocurrency and its monumental influence on the global financial system. This topic may sound high-tech, but we've broken it down into easily digestible pieces that anyone can understand. We explore how this digital revolution is reshaping the money landscape globally, from daily transactions to long-term investments. Whether you're a financial analyst or just curious about what the buzz around 'crypto' means, this report has got you covered. Expect illuminating insights that can help you navigate these new financial waters with confidence. So, why not give it a read and propel yourself into the future of money today?

Chapter 2. The Dawn of Cryptocurrency: A Brief History

In 2008, the world economy plummeted into a catastrophic meltdown that shattered financial institutions and felled gigantic international conglomerates. Amid this upheaval, on a popular cryptography mailing list, an intimate yet entirely anonymous individual or group using the pseudonym 'Satoshi Nakamoto' posted 'Bitcoin: A Peer-to-Peer Electronic Cash System', a white paper that introduced the concept of a new digital currency, Bitcoin.

2.1. A Modest Beginning

Nakamoto's idea wasn't immediately acclaimed or noticed; instead, it slowly began to gain followers. Just over two months after Nakamoto's white paper was published, the first-ever transaction in Bitcoin was made between Nakamoto and Hal Finney, a developer and early cryptocurrency enthusiast. This event was the beginning of a new era, even if it was then unrecognized.

In January 2009, Nakamoto mined the first block of the Bitcoin blockchain — the indispensable foundation of the cryptocurrency — dubbed the "Genesis Block" or "Block 0". This action opened up a new chapter in currency history that now ripples across the global economy.

2.2. Cryptocurrency Exchanges and Bitcoin Pizza Day

As the idea of Bitcoin began to spread and the number of

transactions increased, there was an apparent need for a platform to trade this new digital currency. In March 2010, the first such platform, BitcoinMarket.com, began operations, with the price of Bitcoin was around $0.003. Fast-forward to May 22, 2010, a day now celebrated as Bitcoin Pizza Day. On this day, Laszlo Hanyecz, an early Bitcoin miner, traded 10,000 Bitcoins for two pizzas, the first documented purchase of a product with the new digital currency. In present-day value, this would be worth millions of dollars.

2.3. Enter the Altcoins

By 2011, Bitcoin had sparked a revolution, giving birth to the idea of creating similar digital currencies. This year marked the emergence of various types of cryptocurrency, known collectively as Altcoins. Among the earliest Altcoins are Namecoin, Litecoin, and SwiftCoin. Each came with its own unique features, innovations, and focus areas.

From 2012 to 2013, Bitcoin transactions multiplied rapidly, with more and more people and institutions seeing its potential. However, Bitcoin also became associated with illegal transactions, especially on the dark web, leading to increased scrutiny from law enforcement agencies worldwide.

In November 2013, Bitcoin reached $1,000 for the first time. This valuation was an acknowledgment of its growing influence and the burgeoning interest in cryptocurrencies on a broader scale.

2.4. Rise of Ethereum and Smart Contracts

In 2014, 19-year-old Vitalik Buterin, a programmer, and cryptocurrency enthusiast, introduced a new blockchain project called Ethereum. Unlike Bitcoin, or any of its contemporaries,

Ethereum offered a new concept: Smart Contracts. These dynamic contracts run on the blockchain and execute when their conditions are met, bringing a whole new layer of functionality to the blockchain technology.

This introduction of Smart Contracts triggered a new wave of innovation and development. It opened the doors for the creation and implementation of Decentralized Applications (DApps), which operate directly on the blockchain, eliminating the need for a central point of control, thus further diffusing power away from central entities and towards individuals.

In 2015, the Ethereum network finally went live. Its native digital currency, Ether, has been one of the most valuable cryptocurrencies by market capitalization, second only to Bitcoin.

2.5. The ICO Boom and Crypto Winter

With Smart Contracts came the Initial Coin Offering (ICO) boom. Numerous projects started raising capital via ICOs, where they issued their own tokens in exchange for widely accepted cryptocurrencies like Bitcoin or Ether. The year 2018 saw a massive burst of ICO activity.

However, intense speculation and questionable projects led to the ICO bubble bursting, leading to what is known as the Crypto Winter in late 2018. Most cryptocurrencies suffered major losses, and the market sentiment took a drastic toll.

Despite the Crypto Winter, the ecosystem was far from dead. Instead, it led to a thorough cleanup of the crypto landscape. This period led to the demise of projects that lacked substance and allowed those with real potential, robust technology, and use-cases to stay afloat and further develop.

2.6. The Status Quo

As of now, the cryptocurrency market has rebounded splendidly from its slumber, reaching new all-time highs. Bitcoin crossed the $60,000 mark in 2021, underlining its increasing mainstream acceptance. Institutions are embracing cryptocurrencies, with businesses like Tesla investing heavily in Bitcoin, and payment platforms like PayPal allowing cryptocurrencies as a viable payment method. Governments are also wading into the crypto waters, with countries like China developing their own digital currencies.

From an obscure concept floated by an anonymous individual in a niche mailing list to a revolutionary technology influencing all sectors of the global economy, the journey of cryptocurrency has been tumultuous and electrifying. However, it is clear that the Dawn of Cryptocurrency has undoubtedly ended with its position cemented, not as an alternative, but as a major player in the global financial system. It is now up to us to see how well we can adapt to this new epoch.

Chapter 3. Understanding the Basics: Bitcoin, Blockchain and Beyond

Cryptocurrency. This digital 'stuff' that has been jumping off the charts in recent years, provoking both awe and anxiety in equal measure. Some deem it as a dangerous financial bubble, while others view it as the next gold rush - a phenomenon shaping a radically new paradigm in the world economy. The foundational pillar of that revolution is Bitcoin, built on a technology known as Blockchain. Understanding these terms and their intrinsic associations is crucial when exploring the labyrinth of cryptocurrency.

3.1. What is Bitcoin?

Often symbolized as BTC, Bitcoin is the first cryptocurrency created. It was introduced in 2009 by an unidentified persona (or group) under the pseudonym Satoshi Nakamoto. Unlike currencies we're used to like the Dollar, Euro or Yen, Bitcoin has no physical presence. Its existence resides purely online.

The idea behind Bitcoin was to create a currency that doesn't depend on any central authority and could be sent electronically in a secure, verifiable and immutable way. It functions on a decentralized system, with transactions maintained on a public ledger called the blockchain.

Bitcoin can be divided into smaller units known as "satoshis", with one bitcoin equalling 100 million satoshis.

3.2. Bitcoin Transactions: No Middlemen Required

Bitcoin works under a peer-to-peer network, where transaction details are directly communicated between parties, without the intervention of any external institution like a bank.

When Alice wants to send 1 Bitcoin to Bob, she creates a message (transaction) signed with her private cryptographic key. This encoded message includes the sender's and receiver's public keys (Bitcoin addresses) and the amount being transferred.

This transaction isn't immediately finalized, though. It's broadcasted to the Bitcoin network and waits for confirmation. This process is handled by a unique and sophisticated system built on blockchain technology.

3.3. Blockchain: A Revolutionary Ledger

Blockchain, at its core, is a kind of decentralized ledger that maintains transaction details in a series of interlocked data units called "blocks". The term 'blockchain' originates from the method how these blocks are connected in a chain-like manner.

Each block contains several transactions and once it reaches its data limit, a new block is created. They are linked using unique identifiers known as 'hashes', cryptographic codes produced by algorithms.

A key feature of blockchain is its decentralized nature. Instead of a single entity controlling the data, dozens, hundreds, or potentially even thousands of computers (called nodes) participate in the upkeep of the blockchain. They validate and record transactions continuously and independently.

This leads to a high level of transparency and resilience. It's almost impossible to alter or falsify the data already written on the blockchain owing to the consensus mechanism, which makes it a robust and secure method for recording transactions.

3.4. Into the Mines: Understanding Bitcoin Mining

Bitcoin mining has nothing to do with excavating earth. It is the process of verifying Bitcoin transactions and recording them onto the blockchain. It's how new bitcoins are introduced into circulation and how the Bitcoin network is secured.

Competing to solve complex mathematical puzzles, miners use high computational power. The first to solve it gets to place the next block on the blockchain and is rewarded with a quantity of newly created bitcoins and transaction fees. This is the only way to generate new bitcoins - often likened to gold mining, from which the term 'Bitcoin mining' is derived.

3.5. Bitcoin's Monetary Policies: Finite Supply and Halving

A fundamental rule in Bitcoin's code is that only 21 million bitcoins will ever exist. This absence of an unlimited supply makes Bitcoin a deflationary currency, unlike traditional currencies which central banks can mint unlimited quantities leading to inflation.

Another distinctive policy is the Bitcoin halving event - a pre-programmed function in the Bitcoin protocol that cuts the block reward to miners in half approximately every four years. It's an economic paradigm to ensure that Bitcoin's supply doesn't deplete too quickly.

3.6. Privacy, Security, and Control: Key Features of Bitcoin

Bitcoin provides end-users with enhanced privacy compared to traditional financial operations. No personal data is linked with the Bitcoin wallet addresses, ensuring privacy. However, it's worth noting that all transaction details are public, resulting in a pseudonymous state where Bitcoin addresses aren't tied to identities but could potentially be linked back through analysis or transaction tracking.

Moreover, owning Bitcoin offers full control over financial assets without the need for intermediaries. However, it also requires the user to secure private keys responsibly. Without backup or recovery, a lost private key implies that the associated Bitcoins are forever lost.

In conclusion, Bitcoin is an innovative digital currency that is decentralized, provably scarce, and offers an unprecedented level of monetary autonomy. Its underlying technology, blockchain, is viewed as a significant disruptor in numerous fields beyond finance, and its potential is being explored globally.

Chapter 4. Current Impact: Crypto's Role in Today's Financial Market

Cryptocurrencies, with Bitcoin at the forefront, have started to make a significant impact on the global financial markets. These digital currencies are shaping the way transactions are done, investments are made, and fortunes accumulated. The growth of cryptocurrencies has been explosive, particularly in the last five years, prompting increased interest and spurring comprehensive discussions among regulators, investors, and financial institutions worldwide.

4.1. The Advent of Cryptocurrencies

Brought into existence by a person (or group) known as Satoshi Nakamoto in 2009, Bitcoin represented a new form of unregulated virtual currency. The underlying technology of blockchain, a decentralized ledger that records all transactions, provided for a secure, transparent, and democratic form of digital cash.

The core promise of cryptocurrencies is their decentralized nature. No single individual, organization, or government can control them - the 'crypto' community collectively manages these digital currencies. This level of financial freedom had not been achieved before. Consequently, cryptocurrencies have rapidly gained popularity, particularly amongst those wary of traditional banking systems and governmental financial management.

4.2. Mainstream Adoption

Today, cryptocurrencies are moving from the periphery into the mainstream. Major businesses like Microsoft, Starbucks, and Tesla accept Bitcoin as payment. Financial service giants like Visa and Mastercard have begun to allow cryptocurrencies on their networks, and numerous bitcoin ATMs have been deployed worldwide. Cryptocurrencies have transcended their original "anarcho-capitalist" vision and are now recognized as legitimate financial assets.

This mainstream adoption has far-reaching implications for the financial world. Cryptocurrencies provide a degree of financial inclusion that the traditional banking system can't match—those without access to commonly used financial institutions can participate in the global economy through cryptocurrencies. This mass inclusion could potentially revolutionize the global economy, putting power back into the hands of the people and stimulating economic growth in otherwise stagnant areas.

4.3. Cryptocurrencies as an Investment Vehicle

Cryptocurrencies have also emerged as a lucrative investment opportunity. The astronomical growth of Bitcoin and other digital coins has yielded outstanding returns for those who invested early. This surge in price has led many investors, both institutional and retail, to consider adding cryptocurrencies to their portfolios.

However, as with all investments, cryptocurrencies come with risks. The cryptocurrency market is notoriously volatile, with prices capable of making extreme swings in a short period. There are concerns over regulatory uncertainties, technological deficiencies, and potential market manipulation. While these digital assets offer sky-high potential returns, investors must be prepared to weather the storms of this often turbulent market.

4.4. Regulatory Implications

The adoption of cryptocurrencies presents a plethora of regulatory implications. Lawmakers and regulators worldwide grapple with how to treat these digital assets. They've to consider consumer protection, anti-money laundering efforts, tax collection, and economic stability.

Yet, the decentralized nature of cryptocurrencies makes them hard to regulate. Without a centralized entity to oversee, it is difficult for a government to exert any control over it. Plus, digital currencies transcend national borders, making regulation even more complicated. This lack of regulation is not only concerning for governments but also for investors who lack the protection typically afforded to other types of assets.

Nevertheless, certain countries have made strides in crypto regulation. Countries such as Singapore and Switzerland have taken crypto-friendly regulatory approaches, capitalizing on the booming market. Others, like China and India, have taken a more conservative stance, issuing bans and restrictions.

4.5. Future Outlook

The future of cryptocurrencies is still unfolding. Increasingly, they are being recognized as a new asset class by investment banks and hedge funds. This mainstream acceptance, combined with advancements in blockchain technology, is likely to spur further adoption.

Despite this positive outlook, the threats posed by regulatory crackdowns, market volatility, and macroeconomic factors are real. Whether or not cryptocurrencies can navigate these challenges and become the norm rather than the exception remains to be seen.

Looking ahead, cryptocurrencies have the potential to revolutionize the financial industry. If blockchain technology and digital currencies continue to evolve and adapt as they have thus far, traditional forms of finance may need to adjust or risk becoming obsolete. The disruption that results could be monumental, changing the market forces that control global finance today.

Chapter 5. Disruption and Innovation: Crypto vs Traditional Banking

The monumental emergence of cryptocurrency has led to a transformative shift in the conventional banking ecosystem. This is a paradigm shift in the financial sector that has hosted noteworthy disruptions and innovations.

5.1. The Birth of a New Financial Order

Cryptocurrencies, often referred to as 'digital gold,' have ushered in a new era of innovation reshaping the traditional concept of money and finance. Born from a need for decentralization, sovereignty from governing authorities, and the desire for confidential transactions, cryptocurrencies have emerged as a serious contender to the traditional banking model.

The operation model of cryptocurrencies is fundamentally different from traditional banking. Cryptocurrencies operate on a technology called 'blockchain,' a decentralized system that distributes transactional information across various computers, ensuring security, transparency, and enhanced tracing ability. This disrupts the centuries-old model of centralized banking, which has been subject to criticism for its opacity and susceptibility to corruption or monetary misuse.

5.2. The Tech Behind the Transformation

The blockchain functions around a decentralized ledger, where every transaction is recorded publicly. This provides a high level of transparency and security, allowing users to track their transactions while maintaining anonymity. The complex cryptographic functions used in these networks render counterfeit or double-spending nearly impossible, thereby challenging the traditional systems where fraudulent activities have their place.

Cryptocurrencies function in a trustless environment – one does not need to trust the other party or a central authority to ensure transaction accuracy. This code-based trust comes in stark contrast with traditional banking, where trust is institutionally mandated and protocol-driven, highlighting a significant disrupter in the banking domain.

5.3. Redefining Transactional Efficiency

Cryptocurrencies have proved to be a game-changer in terms of transactional efficiency. Unlike traditional banking systems, which are restricted by working hours, geographical limitations, and lengthy procedures, crypto transactions are instantaneous, providing round-the-clock services regardless of geographical location. This immediate processing is significant in an increasingly digitized global environment, demanding speed and efficiency.

Crypto streamlines international transactions that are traditionally cumbersome due to currency conversions, banking procedures, and transfer fees. With crypto, transactions become borderless, having the ability to cater to the two billion unbanked population globally. Cryptocurrencies are considered less discriminatory and more inclusive, leading to equality in financial accessibility.

5.4. Challenging the Economic Power Structures

The conventional banking system typically revolves around the central authority's monetary control. These institutions hold the power to print currency and control the flow of money, simultaneously determining inflation rates. This autonomy of centralized banks has often been a topic of controversy, triggering economic debates.

Cryptocurrencies, in their essence, challenge this power structure. The value of crypto is driven purely by supply and demand dynamics. Typically, most cryptocurrencies have a finite supply, mitigating the risk of inflation. Furthermore, cryptocurrencies cannot be manipulated by government institutions, offering resistance against inflation. This has made cryptocurrencies a favored asset class, especially in inflation-stricken economies.

5.5. Risks and Challenges Needing Address

Despite their transformative potential, cryptocurrencies also pose substantial risks and challenges that cannot be overlooked. The volatile nature of cryptocurrencies has led to significant price fluctuations, generating skepticism among potential investors. The unregulated nature of cryptocurrencies and their potential for misuse are prevalent concerns. Another challenge for cryptocurrencies is the lack of widespread acceptance. While many businesses have started to accept crypto as payment, it is merely computing to the acceptance level of conventional currency.

The attribute of anonymity, while being a unique selling point of cryptocurrencies, also doubles as a massive liability. It can potentially facilitate illegal activities, such as money laundering or financing illicit actions. Additionally, the complexity of the technology behind cryptocurrencies provides a steep learning curve for the average consumer.

5.6. Consequences and Potential Impacts of Crypto-Adoption

The increasing rates of crypto-adoption may lead to substantial shifts in economic power dynamics and the financial market. It might pave the way for capital controls to lose their grip on money movements, creating an avenue for more free economic activity. The global acceptance of cryptocurrencies may also further digitize economies, creating more robust digital infrastructure and revolutionizing industries beyond finance.

While the transformation of the banking system through cryptocurrency is undeniable, it does not suggest the extinction of conventional banking. Rather, it could lead to the evolution of traditional banks into more technologically advanced institutions, integrating crypto into their operation models.

In conclusion, cryptocurrencies, with their innovative technology and disruptive properties, have kick-started a revolution that challenges the core of traditional banking. With this, the landscape of finance and banking is on the brink of a major transformation. The coexistence and competition between crypto and banks signal a healthy maturation of the financial ecosystem as both face challenges and advantageous opportunities. The interplay between crypto and traditional banking serves as a testament to economic advancement toward transparent, efficient, and inclusive financial systems.

Chapter 6. The Regulatory Landscape: Governing Crypto around the World

To understand how governments globally are responding to the rise of cryptocurrencies, one must first appreciate the complex interplay between technology, finance, and regulation. Balancing innovation with security considerations, the regulatory landscape is multifaceted and continually evolving - quite similar to the field it supervises.

6.1. The Role of Regulatory Authorities

Regulatory authorities across the globe have varied roles and responsibilities, sometimes extending beyond the traditional remit. As the advent of cryptocurrencies threatens to disrupt traditional financial systems, these authorities are repurposing exisiting rules as well as drafting new ones as the situation demands. Key among their goals is the protection of investors, prevention of fraud, and maintaining the stability of the financial system.

These authorities, ranging from central banks to Securities and Exchange Commissions, are tasked with overseeing the unstable, fast-paced digital currency terrain. They grapple with a broad array of concerns – from ensuring cryptocurrencies aren't used in illicit practices, to devising guidelines for institutions that seek to treat cryptocurrencies as legitimate investment vehicles.

6.2. The United States: A Piecemeal Approach

Looking at the United States, one may observe a somewhat fragmented regulatory landscape. Differing interpretations of whether cryptocurrencies should be classified as securities, commodities, or a new asset class altogether have led to a mix of rules.

The IRS considers cryptocurrency as property, subjecting it to capital gains tax. On the other hand, the Commodity Futures Trading Commission (CFTC) views them as commodities, exerting influence over derivatives markets. Meanwhile, the SEC has been defining the scope of its authority, increasingly scrutinizing initial coin offerings (ICOs) and differentiating between utility tokens and security tokens.

In recent years, attempts have been made to standardize the cryptocurrency regulatory framework at the Federal level. However, such action is often taken reactively, as opposed to proactively, leading to an uncertain environment for those operating in this space.

6.3. European Union: Balancing Ridigity and Innovation

In the European Union, cryptocurrencies are viewed more favorably, and there's a degree of regulatory uniformity because member countries are bound by directives issued by the European Commission. The focus in Europe typically emphasizes fostering innovation while protecting the economy and consumers from potential harm.

EU authorities have been active, albeit cautious, in their approach. With the 5th Anti-Money Laundering Directive (5AMLD), they enforced stringent KYC procedures on crypto exchanges and wallet providers. Simultaneously, entities such as the European Securities and Markets Authority (ESMA) have provided detailed advice to institutions seeking to issue 'crypto-assets.' As a result, countries like Malta and Luxembourg have been able to flourish as blockchain and crypto-friendly hubs.

6.4. China: Tight Reins

China, a country known for its tightly regulated financial sector, has adopted a stricter stance towards cryptocurrencies. The Chinese government has banned cryptocurrency exchanges and ICOs, citing concerns of financial stability and social order. However, the country continues to dominate the global bitcoin mining network, and the central bank is actively developing its own digital currency, the digital yuan.

6.5. Smaller Nations: Cryptocurrency Havens

Smaller nations—such as Malta, Switzerland, and Singapore—have adopted a comparatively relaxed stance. These countries view cryptocurrencies as an opportunity for economic diversification and growth, and thus have established detailed regulatory and legal frameworks to encourage blockchain and cryptocurrency businesses to set up operations.

6.6. Regulatory Sandbox: An Experiment

A noteworthy initiative adopted by several regulatory systems worldwide is the 'regulatory sandbox', an experimental space where businesses can test innovative products, services, and business models without immediately enduring the normal regulatory consequences. The United Kingdom's Financial Conduct Authority was among the first to introduce such a concept.

6.7. The Road Ahead: Standardization

The fragmented nature of cryptocurrency regulations worldwide indicates that there's a long road to achieving a standardized global regulatory approach. The rapid innovation in the crypto landscape paired with its decentralized nature presents challenges to integration. Nevertheless, it's clear that regulators worldwide are actively seeking ways to provide a harmonized approach that balances risk management with fostering innovation.

In conclusion, understanding the regulatory landscape of cryptocurrencies is no simple feat. As countries grapple with this new frontier, the regulations will continue to be as dynamic as the industry itself. With monitoring and adapting being the only constants, knowing the rules of the game becomes invaluable for individuals, businesses, and governments navigating the crypto world.

Chapter 7. Transaction Revolutionized: The Paradigm Shift in Payments

One of the most prominent and impactful ways the advent of cryptocurrency has shifted the financial landscape is through transactions and payment methods. For centuries, exchanges of goods and services have depended on physical currency, checks, and later, digital banking systems. But the latter, while a stepping stone towards modern options, are still often encumbered by delays, fees, and geographical restrictions. Cryptocurrency, with its decentralized and borderless nature, introduces a new approach to transactions, altering the landscape of the finance industry altogether.

7.1. Decentralization and Immediate Settlement

Cryptocurrencies like Bitcoin, Ethereum, and several others are underpinned by blockchain technology, which provides a decentralized and secure method of validating transactions. Unlike traditional financial systems where a central authority such as a bank or government controls and processes transactions, cryptocurrencies are managed by a network of peer-to-peer computers. When a transaction is made, it's broadcast to this network, where it's verified and recorded on a 'block,' then added to the 'chain' of transaction records. This process removes the need for intermediaries, thus reducing costs and transaction times significantly.

Decentralized systems also provide immediate settlement. Settling assets can sometimes take days in traditional banking systems, especially for cross-border transactions. Cryptocurrencies, however, enable users to transfer assets almost instantly, as long as the network processes the transaction. This immediacy can be particularly beneficial for businesses and individuals who require swift transactions.

7.2. Accessibility and Financial Inclusion

One of the most compelling aspects of cryptocurrency is its potential to promote financial inclusion. Traditional banking systems have often been criticized for leaving out a significant part of the world's population. According to the World Bank, around 1.7 billion adults worldwide are unbanked, meaning they don't have access to a bank account or any financial services.

Cryptocurrency proposes a solution to this problem. Given that crypto transactions only require an internet connection, individuals from all walks of life, irrespective of their geographical location, can partake in the digital economy. This, in turn, empowers the unbanked and underbanked, providing them with viable alternatives to access financial services previously unavailable to them, and fostering economic growth globally.

7.3. Reducing Transaction Costs

Much of trading and transaction costs in the traditional financial sector come from intermediaries. These costs can prove prohibitive for many, especially for those who need to complete small transactions frequently. Crypto transactions, on the other hand, eliminate intermediaries from the validation process. As peer-to-peer transactions, the fees are usually minimal, making crypto transactions more cost-efficient. It doesn't matter if you transfer a large sum of money or just a few dollars; the fee doesn't scale with the amount.

This can be especially beneficial to businesses, given the potential for sustained and significant cost savings over time. For microtransactions or cross-border transactions that would otherwise incur high fees, cryptocurrency presents a practical, cost-effective alternative.

7.4. Cross-Border Transactions

One of the particular strengths of crypto lies in its effectiveness in handling cross-border transactions. Moving money across borders involves hefty fees and prolonged waiting periods when handled by traditional banking systems or money transfer services. Cryptocurrencies, by their very nature, are not confined by geographical boundaries. They allow instant and direct transactions between parties, no matter where they are in the world. No need for currency conversion, no need for middleman fees.

This can revolutionize international commerce and remittances, as well as promote personal autonomy over finances. For people working in foreign countries and sending money back home, the provision for low-cost, fast cross-border transactions can make a substantial difference.

While the possibilities of cryptocurrencies seem exciting and promising, they are not without their challenges. Despite the advantages, a total shift in the transactional paradigm also brings up concerns about regulation, security, and financial stability. The potential effects on the economic and political structures that exist around the legacy financial systems are significant and can't be ignored. Therefore, fostering a balanced approach that embraces advancements while addressing potential concerns is essential to propelling this revolutionary innovation forward efficiently and responsibly.

The burgeoning cryptocurrency revolution has undeniably begun to redesign the fabric of the global financial system. It is essential, now more than ever, to understand, engage with, and navigate these changes proactively. The new era of transactions swings the gate open to a more inclusive, efficient, and autonomous financial world. Will it completely replace traditional methods? Only time will tell. But for now, the shift is underway, heralding a promising future for finance as we know it.

Chapter 8. Investment Strategy: Navigating the Crypto Market

Before we venture into the nitty-gritty of crypto investment strategy, it's crucial to grasp that this emerging field isn't just about Bitcoin, Ethereum or individual crypto assets. It is, in fact, a new and rapidly developing market ecosystem. Investing harnesses the successful evolution of this ecosystem, and it isn't merely about picking the next hot token. With that understanding as our stepping stone, let's delve deeper into navigating the crypto market.

8.1. Understanding the Cryptocurrency Market

The first step in developing an effective crypto investment strategy is understanding the market. Cryptoassets are traded on digital exchanges, similar to stock exchanges. The significant difference is that the crypto market never sleeps; it operates 24/7, globally.

Observe the market trends and stay updated with news about various currencies. Watch for high and low trends because they offer insight into the market's volatility. For instance, in December 2017, Bitcoin reached a high of nearly $20,000 only to fall below $4,000 in the following year. This sort of volatility, while not surprising in the crypto world, shocks traditional investors unfamiliar with the landscape.

8.2. Risk Assessment

Cryptocurrency investment is inherently risky, but this doesn't mean the risk is unmanageable. It's crucial to understand that while high-risk may equal high reward, it can also result in significant losses. Before investing, ask yourself how much you're willing to lose without it affecting your quality of life. This will help determine your risk tolerance and guide your investment choices.

While setting up your portfolio, ensure not to put all your eggs in one basket. Cryptocurrency is highly unpredictable, and it's best to diversify your investment across several assets.

8.3. Portfolio Diversification

While it may be tempting to invest in one digital asset that shows promise, a wise crypto investment strategy involves diversifying your portfolio. This, as the adage goes, prevents you from 'putting all your eggs in one basket'. Diversification isn't just about splitting your investment between Bitcoin and Ethereum. Explore smaller, growing cryptocurrencies (often called altcoins) too.

However, diversification doesn't mean investing in every coin that you come across. Take your time to research about these assets—understand their purpose, their team, their technology, and their value proposition.

8.4. Building a Balanced Portfolio

Building a balanced portfolio helps to manage risk and reward. Typically, investors buy a mix of low and high-risk assets. Major cryptocurrencies like Bitcoin and Ethereum are considered to be relatively 'safe' assets. Still, they offer lower potential returns when compared with smaller, more volatile altcoins. Balancing your portfolio with a mix of these assets can help spread the risk while offering the possibility of substantial returns.

8.5. Research and Analysis

Knowledge is, without doubt, your most valuable tool when navigating the crypto market. Many valuable free resources provide comprehensive information about different digital assets. Utilize these resources to learn about the tokens' history, their technology, their team, potential disruptiveness in the ecosystem, and much more.

Investors use several analysis methods to comprehend market trends and guide their investment decisions. Technical Analysis (TA) involves the study of past market data, primarily price and volume, utilising various chart-based techniques to predict future market behavior. Fundamental Analysis (FA) assesses a token's intrinsic value by examining all aspects of the cryptocurrency, including its technology, its team, and more.

To predict market trends and identify potential investment opportunities, seasoned investors use a combination of FA and TA. Keep in mind that while no method is foolproof, a well-reasoned analysis can improve your chances of making successful investments.

8.6. Consistent Monitoring of Portfolio

Another critical aspect of cryptocurrency investing is routine portfolio monitoring. Since crypto markets are notoriously volatile, regular check-ins can help you stay on top of your investments. However, remember to avoid compulsive checking. Whilst it's important to stay updated, continually watching every market fluctuation might trigger panic-selling or unnecessary buying.

8.7. Conclusion: Patience and Persistence

Cryptocurrency investments are rarely get-rich-quick schemes; at least, they shouldn't be. Patience and persistence are essential virtues in the world of crypto investment. There may be moments of exponential growth where temptation to sell runs high, and periods of decline where fear can compel you to sell at a loss. But remember, achieving steady gains over time should be the objective.

In conclusion, the upcoming years are looking promising for the crypto market. With mindful investment strategies and careful market navigation, you have the potential to realize significant growth and gains. Investing wisely with a keen understanding of the landscape and risks involved will give you a solid footing in the exciting world of cryptocurrency.

Chapter 9. Crypto-Security: Safeguarding Your Digital Assets

The inherent nature of cryptocurrencies, with decentralization at its core, calls for a unique set of security considerations. As a participant in this new economy, it's crucial to understand what security measures exist, how to implement them, and why they are so important.

9.1. Understanding Crypto-Security

When dealing with cryptocurrency, the term 'crypto-security' refers to the safeguarding measures designed to protect your digital assets from threats such as hacking, fraud, and technical failures. With a wide range of attack vectors possible in the digital spectrum, security is a cornerstone of any serious crypto endeavour.

9.2. The Importance of Secure Wallets

When operating within the realm of digital currency, a 'wallet' is essentially your bank account. It is how users store, send, and receive cryptocurrency. However, unlike traditional banking systems, if you lose access to your wallet, it can be permanently inaccessible — there are no customer service calls that can retrieve your lost password. This is where the security of your wallet is absolutely vital.

Digital wallets come in several forms — from hardware wallets that can be as small as a USB stick, web-based wallets, desktop software, and even mobile apps. Each of these has its own security considerations.

Hardware wallets are considered the most secure, as they store your assets offline, thus eliminating many potential online threats. Also, even if the hardware is lost or stolen, it can be backed up using a confidential recovery phrase.

Web wallets and other software based wallets offer a blend of convenience and security. Although they are not as impervious to attacks as hardware wallets, they use a variety of encryption techniques to secure your assets. It is vital, however, to use reputable wallet providers and ensure your device's security is robust enough to ward off malware and phishing attacks.

9.3. Keys and Passwords

Safeguarding your cryptocurrency also hinges on the management of your private keys and passwords. A private key is a cryptographic code that allows a user to access their cryptocurrency. A public key, on the other hand, is used to ensure you are the rightful owner of an address that can receive funds.

Keeping your private keys secret and secure is one of the most important security aspects to consider when dealing with cryptocurrencies. If anyone else gets hold of your private key, they can access and transfer your digital coins as if they were theirs.

Password security is also crucial for accessing wallets and exchanges. Implementing strong, unique passwords is highly recommended, along with changing them regularly. Additionally, multi-factor authentication serves to add another layer of security.

9.4. Understanding Blockchain

Due to the widespread adoption of blockchain technology within the crypto sphere, understanding its security implications is paramount. A blockchain is fundamentally a public, encrypted ledger of transactions. While blockchain is seen as inherently secure due to its decentralization and immutability, vulnerabilities do exist.

For instance, a 51% attack is possible where an entity gains control of the majority of a network's mining power. While unlikely, it is technically feasible. As a result, choosing to engage with well-established cryptocurrencies that have vast and distributed networks reduces this risk.

9.5. Safe Trading Practices

Trading cryptocurrencies also poses threats if not carried out securely. Ensure you use reputable exchanges, and try to withdrawal your coins to your secure, private wallet as soon as possible. Leaving coins on an exchange unnecessarily exposes them to potential hacks and security breaches.

Furthermore, beware of scams and too-good-to-be-true investments. It's important to conduct your due diligence when entering any new venture or engaging with new crypto service providers.

9.6. Disaster Recovery

In the event of a disaster, be it a lost wallet or a forgotten password, having recovery measures in place can be crucial. Hardware wallets are commonly backed up by recovery phrases – a set of words that can restore access to your funds. Meanwhile, services such as Google Authenticator provide backup codes for two-factor authentication setups.

In a nutshell, crypto security revolves around keeping your digital assets safe from numerous threats like hacking and phishing attacks. This involves securing wallets, managing keys and passwords, understanding blockchain vulnerabilities, adopting safe trading practices, and having disaster recovery measures. While the ownership and transfer of cryptocurrencies may seem intimidating due to these security considerations, they are manageable. The substantial benefits of crypto, such as swift transactions, reduced fees, and the potential for high returns, make them hard to ignore in the current financial landscape.

Chapter 10. The Future Forecasted: Trends and Predictions in Cryptocurrency

Cryptocurrency, since its inception, has introduced a paradigm shift in the way we perceive and transact money. Over the past decade, cryptocurrency has evolved from a relatively obscure and misunderstood medium to a viable investment product and potential global currency. Let's delve deeper into what the future might hold for this transformative technology.

10.1. Shaping a Decentralized Financial Future

Eliminating the need for intermediaries is a key benefit of blockchain, the underlying technology of cryptocurrencies. A decentralized financial system allows for peer-to-peer transactions, causing dizzying reconfigurations of how we view traditional banking and financial structures. This could potentially disrupt existing banking systems and monopolized financial services industries.

Decentralized Finance, or 'DeFi,' is an emerging trend that could significantly influence cryptocurrency's future. This system shifts financial transactions onto decentralized networks, offering financial services such as lending and borrowing to everyone with internet access, not tied to their physical location or economic status.

10.2. Cryptocurrency as a Global Currency

Bitcoin and other cryptocurrencies have the potential to become a global currency, solving problems associated with different exchange rates and fluctuating currencies. As global commerce and digital transactions become the norm, cryptocurrencies could provide a seamless and universal method of payment, transcending national borders.

However, for this to happen, governments, stakeholders, and the broader financial community will have to accept cryptocurrencies. We have already seen several nations, such as El Salvador, adopting Bitcoin as legal tender, indicative of this future trend.

10.3. Regulatory Developments

Regulation is arguably one of the most considerable forces that will shape the future of cryptocurrency. Governments worldwide grapple with finding the sweet spot between enabling innovation and protecting their citizens from potential risks.

In 2021, we witnessed China cracking down on cryptocurrency mining and transactions, citing environmental issues and financial instability. On the other hand, the USA could follow a more relaxed approach, focusing on regulatory clarity and investor protection.

One can expect a wave of regulatory policies worldwide aimed at standardizing practices within the cryptocurrency industry. While the regulations may pose a challenge in the short term, they will ultimately legitimize and streamline the cryptocurrency market, paving the way for greater adoption.

10.4. Increasing Acceptance and Adoption

The widespread acceptance and adoption of cryptocurrency are slow but seemingly inevitable. As digital natives gain more economic influence, the popularity of cryptocurrencies as a mode of transaction, investment, and savings will likely increase.

This expectation is reaffirmed by a rapidly increasing number of traditional entities, such as MasterCard and PayPal, enabling customers to transact and invest in cryptocurrencies. Corporate buy-ins, most notably Tesla's $1.5 billion Bitcoin investment, also hint at growing confidence in the market.

10.5. Rise of Altcoins and Tokenization

Though Bitcoin remains the most known cryptocurrency, the future may witness the rise of other 'Altcoins.' This development has been fueled by unique use-cases provided by different cryptocurrencies. For instance, Ethereum offers smart contract functionality, paving the way for DeFi applications.

Another noteworthy trend is tokenization – the process of representing real-world assets on a blockchain. Tokenization could revolutionize several industries, including real estate, art, and supply chain, ushering in a new era of fractional ownership and transparency.

10.6. Cryptocurrency and Climate Concerns

Cryptocurrencies, particularly those dependent on energy-intensive 'Proof of Work' computation like Bitcoin, face significant environmental criticisms. Sustainable alternatives, such as 'Proof of Stake,' are gaining traction as they consume up to 99% less energy.

Sustainability is likely to become a significant factor in the evolution of cryptocurrencies. We can expect to see greener coins becoming more popular and older cryptocurrencies evolving more efficient energy models.

10.7. Technological Advancements

Boosted by improving technology, cryptocurrency's potential is continually expanding. Developments such as quantum computing could exponentially increase transaction speed and security, reshaping what's possible with cryptocurrencies.

Other emerging technologies like Artificial Intelligence (AI) and Internet of Things (IoT) could also integrate cryptocurrencies more seamlessly into our digital lives, making them a fundamental part of new economic ecosystems.

Predicting the exact trajectory of cryptocurrencies carries a degree of uncertainty, much like the currencies themselves. The landscape is evolving, and new problems and solutions will undoubtedly appear in time. It behooves investors, governments, and all interested parties to closely follow these developments, carefully balancing the risk and reward while carving strategic paths. To resonate with an apt adage, 'the future is here, and it's distributed.' Expect the unexpected, as the future of cryptocurrency is undeniably thrilling.

Chapter 11. Concluding Thoughts: The Road Ahead for Crypto and the Global Financial System

As we come to the conclusion of our special report, we are now ready to forecast the path that crypto is carving in the global financial system. A world where decentralization, transparency, and digitalization take the helm and alter the way we think about and handle money.

11.1. The Paradox of Volatility and Stability

It feels almost paradoxical to predict a coming era of stability based on the performance of cryptocurrencies whose values can swing dramatically in a matter of days, if not hours. Such volatility has led to the perception of crypto assets as being risky. However, like other nascent technologies, this perceived instability is a part of its maturing process.

In comparison, seasoned technologies were once also considered volatile: imagine the early years of automobiles or the internet. Volatility is often an indicator of the underlying market's struggle to accurately price the new technology. As the technology matures and becomes more established, the volatility decreases. We expect this also to be the case with cryptocurrencies: As mass adoption continues and regulatory frameworks are established, we forecast that the volatility will subside, ushering in a new era of stability.

11.2. Regulatory Frameworks in Evolution

The building of a regulatory environment that understands and manages cryptocurrencies is a key part of this stability. The regulatory landscape today is still in flux, with different countries taking varied yet assertive stances on digital currencies.

Countries like Japan have recognized Bitcoin as a legal payment method, while others, like India and China, have imposed restrictions or outright bans. But with the rising influence of cryptocurrencies, governments worldwide realize the relevance of robust and fair regulations. As the regulatory landscape matures, it will provide much-needed stability and legal security for users and investors, benefiting the cryptocurrency market as a whole.

11.3. Acceptance and use in Everyday Life

Bitcoin started as a peer-to-peer electronic cash system, but due to its volatility, it has mostly been used as a store of value or "digital gold." However, other cryptocurrencies, such as stablecoins, which peg their value to traditional assets like the US Dollar, are gaining traction for transactions.

Moreover, with significant businesses like PayPal, Microsoft, and Tesla accepting Bitcoin and other cryptocurrencies as payment, it's not far-fetched to think that crypto could soon become a regular part of our daily transactions and financial interactions. This would redefine the way we think about money, transcending geographical boundaries and traditional banking limitations.

11.4. Long-Term Investment Opportunities

The rising popularity of Initial Coin Offerings (ICOs), Security Token Offerings (STOs), and Decentralized Finance (DeFi) platforms echo the increasing acceptance of crypto as an investment asset class. As adoption rates ascend and perceived risk decreases, more institutional investors are likely to enter the fray, further bolstering the market's maturity and stability.

High-return potential of crypto assets, coupled with advancements in tokenized assets and fractional ownership, presents unprecedented opportunities for both institutional and individual investors. Decentralized exchanges have democratized investing, breaking down barriers to entry such as high minimum investment limits. Such a shift could define a new era of public participation in previously exclusive markets.

11.5. The Role of Blockchain in Financial Institutions

Blockchain, the technology underpinning cryptocurrencies, holds transformative potential beyond supporting digital currencies. Financial institutions are actively exploring blockchain for its capacity to enhance operational efficiencies, improve transparency in transactions, reduce fraud, and cut costs.

The adoption of blockchain technology could fundamentally reshape banking and financial services. Smart contracts, for instance, can automate complex financial transactions, reducing the need for intermediaries and bringing about greater financial inclusion. Thus, blockchain adoption represents another pivotal dimension to consider in the road ahead for crypto and the global financial system.

11.6. Closing Thoughts

In conclusion, the journey of cryptocurrencies from their inception to their current stage has been nothing short of extraordinary. With a global market cap surpassing $2 trillion, cryptocurrencies unquestionably hold great sway over our financial future.

As with any sea change, however, there will be tremors. Volatility, regulatory struggles, fraud, technological learning curves, and general skepticism are all hurdles to be surmounted.

Yet, the potential benefits - decentralization, transparency, efficiency, and financial inclusion, among others - render these challenges worthwhile. As more entities - individuals, enterprises, and governments alike - engage with cryptocurrencies and blockchain technology, the global financial landscape will transform in ways we are just beginning to glimpse.

To stay ahead in this inevitable digital revolution calls for open-mindedness, adaptability, and a willingness to embrace the new dynamics of money. Crypto doesn't claim to be a panacea for the world's financial woes, but it offers a start – and an exciting one at that. Our exploration and understanding of this technology and its potential impacts are still in its early stages, and already, the future looks promising.

As we harness the revolutionary essence of cryptocurrencies, let's remember that we're not just spectators but active participants in this grand reshaping of our global financial order. The road ahead may be challenging, but it's one that leads towards an innovative, inclusive and decentralized future. Let's journey this path together.